MW00596670

A Place Called

Heaven

Dr. Gary L. Wood

A Place Called

Heaven

Dr. Gary L. Wood

Unless otherwise indicated, all Scripture quotations are taken from *The Living Bible*, © 1971. Used by permission of Tyndale House Publishers, Inc., Wheaton, Illinois 60189. All rights reserved. Scripture quotations marked (KJV) are taken from the King James Version of the Holy Bible. Scripture quotations marked (NIV) are taken from the *Holy Bible, New International Version*®, NIV®, © 1973, 1978, 1984 by the International Bible Society. Used by permission of Zondervan. All rights reserved. Scripture quotations marked (NKJV) are taken from the *New King James Version*, © 1979, 1980, 1982, 1984 by Thomas Nelson, Inc. Used by permission. All rights reserved.

Boldface type in the Scripture quotations indicates the author's emphasis.

A Place Called Heaven

RevMedia Publishing
P.O. Box 5172
Kingwood, TX 77325
www.davidyanezministries.com
www.revmediapublishing.com

ISBN: 978-1-62911-199-5
eBook ISBN: 978-1-62911-200-8
Printed in the United States of America
© 2008, 2014 by Dr. Gary L. Wood

Distributed by
Banner Publishing
1030 Hunt Valley Circle
New Kensington, PA 15068

No part of this book may be reproduced or transmitted in any form or by any means, electronic or mechanical—including photocopying, recording, or by any information storage and retrieval system—without permission in writing from the publisher. Please direct your inquiries to permissionseditor@whitakerhouse.com.

2 3 4 5 6 7 8 9 10 11 ฿20 19 18 17 16 15 14

DEDICATION

In Memory of:

Adopted parents
Jessie James Wood and Mary Ruby Wood

Natural parents
Nelson and Joyce Dobbins
(all parents are in heaven)

To my wife, Deena,
who has loyally stood by me

To my children, Angel and David

To my wife's parents,
Mr. & Mrs. Ken Kennedy

PREFACE

How can I project my testimony in a few words? My sudden death in a car accident at eighteen escorted me into a place called heaven. My closest friend, who had died in a tragic accident, was the one chosen to show me around in heaven. Just as I was beginning to make a permanent adjustment, my friend put his hand gently on my shoulder and said, "Gary, you have to go back. She is using that name, Jesus."

My baby sister had been with me in that car accident and I knew instinctively that she was calling me back by using that name. My thoughts were confirmed. After my heavenly tour, things did not look so good in the natural realm. I badly needed plastic surgery and my teeth were to become like stars; they come out at night. I had no vocal cords. Imagine the nurse's startled face when she greeted me, and I answered her back. I have an X-ray that shows that I have no vocal cords, yet I talk and sing.

I sum up a place called heaven with these words. There is a heaven to gain and a hell to shun. Judgment is simply what we have done with Jesus in this life. This is the final battle. We are in the final quest. What is unseen is more real than what is seen.

Fasten your seatbelts and take a journey with me to *A Place Called Heaven.*

Dr. Gary Wood, Th.D.
Grace Theological Seminary

PRAISE

Dear Gary,

Thanks for being such a great brother and disciple of Christ. From the time I was six years old, all I can ever remember you wanting to be is a preacher. When we played in the yard and garage in Dallas, Texas, we played church while the other kids played school. You would be the preacher and I would play the piano. Thanks for staying true to your dream and to Christ. Thank you for all your help, support & prayers.

Love & Blessings

—*Sue Patterson*

Gary Wood has been a friend for over nineteen years. I have had plenty of opportunities to observe him both as a pastor and traveling minister. I have preached for Gary when he forfeited his own check to see that I was properly covered. He shows unusual integrity, and of course, a very effective anointing. Any pastor should feel honored to have Gary Wood as a guest minister in his church.

Sincerely,

—*Dr. Gerald Davis*
Overflowing Cup Ministries International, Inc.
Teaching Seminars Overseas—Evangelism—Special Engagements
New Caney, Texas

May 30, 2001

To all who will hear:

On Easter of this year, our church had the privilege of starting a revival with Rev. Gary Wood and family. For a pastor to allow someone else to take his pulpit on Easter, the greatest day to impact his community requires real trust in another's ministry. The revival was a life changing experience for many. I can say that Rev. Gary Wood is a man of integrity. His ministry will strengthen your faith in heaven. In one of the services, he prayed for people's backs, in an unusual way...I have received numerous reports of sustained healings from that service! Rev. Gary Wood was also asked to minister at our annual Men's Resurrection Breakfast, attended by ten other churches, and at this breakfast nearly thirty men committed their lives to Jesus Christ!

We have a medical doctor that attends our church. He read the X-ray's that Rev. Gary Wood has with him of his accident. He was astounded that Gary is alive, because of the broken vertebrae...one of which causes certain death. I have found that Rev. Gary Wood's life after death experience, to be one of the most "scriptural" in detail.

I do, with conviction, give my recommendation.

In His Service,

—*Pastor Jonathan Mitchell*
Centerburg Church of God, Centerburg, Ohio

It is my privilege to introduce to you Gary, Deena, and Angel Wood.

Gary has a tremendous testimony. He had a horrible automobile accident many years ago. He had a mid-face injury with lorinzal injuries, which means his vocal cords and voice box was completely shattered. He was given no hope to ever talk again by the doctors.

God touched Gary, and he healed him, and now, not only does he preach the Word of God, he also sings. Angel, his daughter, is an equal testimony to God's grace and mercy. I know they will bless your heart.

—*Dr. Paul Osteen,*
Lakewood Church, Houston, Texas

Dr. Gary,

Thank you for your friendship and being a Father in the faith. You and your family are precious to us. I believe your best days are before you.

—*Pastor Jesse DiMartino*
Sarasota, FL.

Gary,

At a time that our lives were totally open to a move of God from heaven, you were sent.

Love,

—*Pastor Jack & Dee Cashman*
York, Pennsylvania

It was 1977 that I met Gary and his precious family at a Business Men's Holy Spirit meeting. I was impressed with his teaching and boldness. After the meeting, I asked you, Gary, to teach a Bible study in our home. You said, "well, maybe one time," and that one time lasted almost twenty years. Your family became our family. You became our spiritual son, along with your family. We love you all dearly.

—*Mama Faerl & Mr. Scooter*
Houston, Texas

Gary & Deena,

You have been such a blessing to us since we met five years ago. We can truly say you are two of our dearest friends. You have always been there to encourage us and without a doubt made us laugh till we hurt.

Love,

—*Pastors Simon & Mary Whatley*
Alvin, Texas

Dear Brother Gary,

I knew you and loved you for twenty-five years before I actually met you. My brother John Greiner gave me a tape of your testimony that I promptly wore out in about two years. I have told your wonderful story to so many people over the years, and you have blessed so many you don't even know about. You will see them in heaven. In the meantime, I can be blessed with fellowship with you and your sweet wife Deena and daughter Angel.

We love you both,

—*Bob & Sylvia Greiner*
San Antonio, Texas

Dear friend, Gary,

It is hard to even put into words how much your friendship and fellowship means to us. You have encouraged us through some dark days, and you have blessed our congregation with your generous and loving ministry. You have made heaven more real to our hearts. We will be eternally grateful that God allowed our paths to cross with you and your precious family. Joy just flows like a river when we are together. We have been through some amazing experiences together. Just one continuous celebration! Bottom line, it's all about Him!

Yours for the cause,

—*Pastors Al & Ruthjoy Capozzi*
Bloomsburg, Pennsylvania

Dear Brother Wood,

Your ministry was a tremendous blessing to King's Cathedral. Thank you so much for investing in our cathedrals in Maui and Oahu. I trust the Lord will continue to use you powerfully this year.

Sincerely,

—*Rev. Brian Reynolds*, Administrative Pastor
cc. Dr. James Marocco, Senior Pastor
Kahului, Maui, Hawaii

To whom it may concern,

I am so pleased for the opportunity to recommend the anointed ministry of Dr. Gary Wood. I have known Gary for more than twenty years, and his character and integrity are beyond reproach. Together with his wife Deena and daughter Angel, he's fought first-hand through life's medical trials and come out victoriously. It is so refreshing to see a minister who lives what he preaches.

I invite Gary to my church regularly, and his preaching is always confirmed with healings, miracles, and salvation. His incredible testimony and riotous sense of humor seem to draw people in almost instantly. Before they realize it, they're delving deeply into God's Word, relating so much to the simple but powerful truths this humble man serves up. He flows with the Holy Spirit and is not afraid to interrupt his message to minister what the Spirit says. People always leave strengthened and encouraged in their faith.

I recommend Dr. Gary Wood to other Pastors enthusiastically and without reservation. Through anointing and example, he leads others in trusting God, no matter what.

Sincerely,

—*Dr. John Greiner*, Pastor
Glorious Way Church, Houston, Texas

FOREWORD

My husband Roger and I have been friends with Gary and Deena for twenty years. Jesus has been the focal point of their lives. They have consistently supported us as their friends and have shown us the Father's love always.

—*Georgeanne Dewitt*, author
New Covenant Praise Church, Houston, Texas

Brother Gary and Sister Deena,

We are truly blessed to have you as friends. You have our respect and admiration in this wonderful journey with the Lord. Your faithfulness in Christ has been an enriched blessing to us, and we honor you and all that you represent. It takes a special person to work as hard as you do for the kingdom of God. Thanks for being such a great example to all of us in ministry.

—*Pastors Simon and Mary Whatley*
Gleaner Full Gospel Church, Alvin, Texas

A NOTE FROM THE AUTHOR

Because I believe that experiences are a dime a dozen, unless they line up with the Word of God, I ask that you would bow your head and pray, asking God to speak to your heart and to confirm the truths of my story. When you read of someone's experience or testimony, you should always test it with the Holy Scriptures. I have been faithful to write and record all that the Lord has shown and told me. You should read this book along with your Bible. (Many of the Scriptures are out of *The Living Bible*.) May Jesus use this book to bring Him glory.

Dear Reader,

You are about to witness, through this book, a living, breathing miracle. I first heard Dr. Gary Wood's astounding testimony while attending a Full Gospel Businessmen's meeting as a young believer more than twenty-five years ago. His account of heaven and the corresponding wonders of resurrection and restoration made an indelible mark on my life. As I played the cassette of his message for family and friends, many were saved; all were changed. Still in my library today, this time-honored report amazes and thrills me as much now as it did then.

All these years later, I am honored to be Dr. Wood's pastor. Beyond his testimony, I can tell you he lives a life of holiness and integrity. He truly carries heaven's touch everywhere God sends him. Let the words of this book change your life like they have mine.

Sincerely,

—*Dr. John W. Greiner*
Pastor, Glorious Way Church, Houston, Texas

A PLACE CALLED HEAVEN

This book is about a place called heaven, a place that I long for to this very day, a place where I did not want to leave. The Lord had a different plan. He sent me back so that I would tell everyone the glorious wonders that await the children of God. Being in heaven was the most awesome experience of my life, and I want to share this incredible story with you. I also want to share one of the most difficult situations I have ever been faced with and that was the day my natural mother called to tell me that my younger half-brother, David, had been killed in a drug raid, and she wanted me to preach at his funeral. Most preachers have reverent things to say about the deceased, but I could not think of anything reverent to say about David.

David was a member of the motorcycle gang, Hell's Angels. Not only did he abuse himself with drugs and alcohol, he abused anyone who got in his way. The day that he was killed, he had beaten our mother to the point of breaking her leg. My brother was not a nice person. The drug raid resulted in gun shots, and when the smoke finally cleared, the police found his body on the floor, dead, not from a gunshot wound, but from a drug overdose. I loved my brother; even so, I believed he had gone to hell.

Losing a loved one is never easy, but if you know that they had asked Jesus into their heart, you can take comfort in knowing that they are in heaven with Jesus. On the other hand, if there is uncertainty, the reality of my knowing that David had chosen to live his life apart from Jesus, and there was no doubt of eternal hell, the sorrow was unbearable. Many people deal with the loss of a loved one who was not saved by dismissing the realization of hell all together. I've heard people say, "I don't believe in a God who would send people to hell." I don't either! God does not send people to hell. You send yourself. You are going to live for eternity. That is a fact. It is your choice, before you leave this earth, whether you will live it in heaven or hell. Jesus warns us of hell two hundred and forty-four times in the Bible. If you were driving down the road and saw two hundred and forty-four warning signs stating that the road ahead was out, would you continue driving in the same direction? Of course not, but you may be living your life, ignoring the warning signs. Maybe you are thinking, *I've never done drugs, beaten my mother; nor have I killed anyone. That is the kind of people who go to hell. I'm a good ol' boy (or gal) compared to them. I've filled out my membership card at the church, been baptized in water, or sprinkled by a priest.*

Well, friend, I am here to tell you that you can be baptized in water until you know every fish by their first name, or sign your name on every church membership in the state, and it is no more effective than shaking a donkey's tail or signing your name on a barn door, unless you have accepted Jesus Christ into your life as your personal Savior. You see, there is no *soul sleeping* or no *purgatory* where you can *hang out* until you find your way to heaven. I know that there are people who believe that you do not have to be saved to go to heaven. Some even claim to have been to heaven, and they say that heaven awaits everyone, no matter how we live our lives and that we don't need Jesus to get there. But that is not what Jesus said. Jesus said, *"Unless you are born again, you can never get into the Kingdom of God"* (John 3:3). This new birth experience is transition from the kingdom of darkness into the *kingdom of light*. It is turning from the ways of the flesh and sin, to the ways of God. We are told of this in Romans, *"Don't copy the behavior and customs of this world, but be a new and different person with a fresh newness in all you do and think"* (Romans 12:2). In Ephesians, the Bible says, *"Live no longer as the unsaved do, for they are blinded and confused"* (Ephesians 4:17).

I have come to recognize that the most profound thought that can ever occupy a person's mind is heaven and how to get there, and the simplest truth you can ever grasp is that Jesus loves you. He will put your sins behind His back as far as the east is from the west, and what is so exciting, is He promises He will never leave us or forsake us. He gives us the power of the Holy Spirit to overcome the enemy, and He provides for us an eternal abode in *A Place Called Heaven*....and I've been there!

I was born on March 1, 1949, in Dallas, Texas. Gary Lynn Dobbins was my given name at birth. Both my mother and father were alcoholics and abusive to me and my little sister, Sue. The Lord Jesus had His hand on our lives. While we were still so small and helpless, my parents decided that their lives would be simpler without the burden of raising Sue and I, so they left us on the porch steps of my maternal grandparents' house. Their name was Wood. My grandparents showed us the kind of love that Christ has for us by adopting us as their own children. Jesus said, *"No, I will not abandon you or leave you as orphans in the storm—I will come to you,"* (John 14:18). God never leaves you. You may walk away from Him, turn your back on Him, but He will not walk away and leave you. I looked up the word *adoption* and found that it meant "being placed as a son into a family, with all the rights and privileges of one bearing the father's name." I can identify with the apostle Paul when he said, *"We should not be like cringing, fearful slaves, but we should behave like God's very own children adopted into the very bosom of his family, and calling to him, 'Abba, Father'"* (Romans 8:15). Abba Father is a very intimate phrase in the Greek language which means Daddy, Daddy or Papa, Papa.

Our family attended Hillcrest Baptist Church on a regular basis. It was there that I heard for the first time, *"For God so loved the world, that he gave his only begotten Son, that whosoever believeth in him should not perish, but have everlasting life"* (John 3:16 KJV). I remember responding to a message my pastor was preaching and walking down the aisle and receiving Jesus Christ as my personal Savior. It was at that moment in which I was adopted into the family of God. *"But to all who receive him, he gave the right to become children of God,"* (John 1:12). All they needed to do was to trust Him to save them. So you see, once you have asked Jesus into your heart, you are instantaneously adopted into the family of God, with all the rights and privileges of a son. *"His unchanging plan has always been to adopt us into his own family by sending Jesus Christ to die for us. And he did this because He wanted to"* (Ephesians 1:5).

On a recent trip to the Holy Land, I learned that a natural born Jewish son can be excommunicated and lose his inheritance, but an adopted child can never lose his inheritance. It is the same with our Heavenly Father. Once you have been adopted into the family of God, your name is written in the Lamb's Book of Life, never to be erased. I am so thankful for a Heavenly Father who will never abandon us. (See 2 Corinthians 4:9.)

Due to economic reasons, my family moved from Dallas, Texas, to Farmington, New Mexico. It was there I met a boy named John who became my best friend and would play a very important role in my life.

At a very young age I began to feel the call of God upon my life. I used to *play* church. I would make pews out of the dining room chairs, and my little sister, Sue, and John would stand up and sing "The Old Rugged Cross" from pretend hymnals, then I would preach. I would high step across the floor, pound on my pulpit, which I had made from a TV tray, just like the hell-fire and brimstone preachers I would hear on Sunday mornings.

As I entered into my high school years, the feeling that God had a call upon my life began to deepen. The Lord blessed me tremendously with the ability to sing His praises, and for three years in a row I won Outstanding Soloist in the state of New Mexico, through all-state competition. It was in my senior year of high school when I was shaken by the devastating news that John had been killed in an automobile accident. I grieved terribly for the loss of my friend. Visions of the accident haunted my dreams for months afterwards.

In 1966, I was a freshman at Wayland Baptist College. I was home for the Christmas holidays. Sue and I had borrowed my grandfather's car and were on our way home from visiting friends. We were just one mile from home and "Silent Night" rang in the air as we sang, when suddenly, her songs of joy turned into a scream of terror.

I turned to see what the matter was. There was an explosion, then a sharp, instant pain seared across my face. There was a brilliant light that engulfed me, and I remember being free from all pain. I slipped out of my body. It was like slipping out of my clothing. I was above the car now; it was as if the top of the car had been removed. I could see my body; I could hear Sue crying. My life passed before my very eyes. I had heard that is what happens. I had never given it much thought. Then again, I was only eighteen years old and had not thought too much about my death. I certainly never thought I would die young. There I was, looking down at my body, seeing my life go by like a rerun. Everything, in just an instant, flashed before me. I had no fear, and there was no sorrow or confusion. I truly believed that I would never return from this experience. I was in a swirling, funnel-shaped cloud that grew wider and wider and brighter and brighter. As I began to ascend up through this tunnel of light, I felt such a tranquil feeling of peace wash over me, wave after glorious wave. At the end of this brilliant tunnel was a pathway. I could see down the path a very bright, yet not blinding light. I was moving and it was like the moving sidewalks in an airport. All around me I could hear angels singing: "Worthy is the Lamb that was slain to receive glory, power, wisdom, and dominion be Thine forever, O Lord, amen and amen." Oh the glory of it! You have never heard anything so beautiful and awesome until you hear the angels singing! Those angelic choruses reverberated off the walls of my soul. It still gives me goose bumps when I think how incredibly beautiful the songs were that I heard the angels sing. I look forward to the glorious day described in the book of Revelation when millions of angels and untold millions of the redeemed will stand before the throne of almighty God, and in unity, sing worship and praise to our Lord Jesus.

> *After this I beheld, and, lo, a great multitude, which no man could number, of all nations, and kindreds, and people, and tongues, stood before the throne, and before the Lamb, clothed with white robes, and palms in their hands; And cried with a loud voice, saying Salvation to our God which sitteth upon the throne, and unto the Lamb. And all the angels stood around about the throne, and about the elders and the four beasts, and fell before the throne on their faces, and worshiped God.*
>
> (Revelation 7:9–11 KJV)

I saw the clouds open up wide. I then began walking on a green, lush carpet of grass that covered the hillside. Looking down, I noticed that the grass came all the way through my feet and that there were no indentions where I had just walked. From the hill, I viewed the outer portion of a magnificent city. There was a wonderful wall made of jasper that surrounded the city. The names of the twelve apostles were inscribed on the foundations. There were twelve pearl gates in the wall, and above each gate the names of the twelve tribes of Israel were engraved. The Bible gives us the dimensions of that city. It is 2.7 billion cubic miles in circumference, 2,250,000 square miles at its base of perimeter, and 780,000 stories high. Can you imagine the dimensions and magnitude of this place called heaven? It has enough rooms to accommodate 100 billion people. That is more than have ever lived on the planet earth at any one time. Jesus said, *"In my Father's house are many mansions"* (John 14:2 KJV).

In front of me was a very beautiful gate made of solid pearl that was studded with sapphires, rubies, diamonds, and many other precious gems. It was the most excellent work of art I have ever seen. The wall was so high that I could not see the top of it. It seemed to go on forever. A giant angel was holding a sword while standing guard at the gate. He was at least forty feet tall. His hair was spun gold. Rays of dazzling, soft lights flowed from this magnificent being. Another angel came through the gate, and he was checking the pages of a book that he was carrying. He then nodded to the giant angel, confirming that I may enter into the city. Suddenly, there in front of me stood my best friend, John. His eyes sparkled with life as we embraced. People have asked me if we will know one another in heaven. I knew my friend John. The Bible says in Mathew 8:11 that we will sit down with Abraham, Isaac, and Jacob. How will we sit down with them if we do not know who they are? The car accident that had taken John's life was so violent that his head had been decapitated. In heaven he is whole. If someone is blind here on earth, when they die, and if they go to heaven, they will be able to see. It is the same if someone is missing arms or legs, when they get to heaven they will be whole and complete. *"When we die and leave these bodies—we will have wonderful new bodies"* (2 Corinthians 5:1), and *"These earthly bodies make us groan* and sigh, but we wouldn't like to think of dying and having no bodies at all. We want to slip into our new bodies so that these dying bodies will, as it were, be swallowed up by everlasting life" (2 Corinthians 5:4), and "Now we look forward with confidence to our heavenly bodies, realizing, that every moment we spend in these earthly bodies is time spent away from our eternal home in heaven with Jesus" (verse 6). I later learned that we are all assigned a loved one, who is already in heaven, to acquaint us to this place called heaven, and John was the one assigned to me.

Yes, what a glorious scene, maybe it's that mother you have missed so much or that baby you lost, your dear father that you laid in the grave, that beloved wife that died of cancer, whoever that loved one may be, if they died in Christ, they will be there to meet you in heaven! John told me he had many wonderful things to show me.

John took me into a very large building that looked like a library. The walls were solid gold and sparkled with a dazzling display of light that loomed up high to a crystal, domed ceiling. I saw hundreds and hundreds of volumes of books. Each book had a cover of beautifully carved gold with a single letter of the alphabet engraved on the outside. Many angels were there reading the contents of the books. John explained to me that these books contain a record of every person's life that has ever been born, throughout all history. Everything we do here on earth is recorded in these books—good or bad—everything. I watched as an angel opened one of the books, and with a cloth, wiped the pages. As he did this, the page turned red and the writing vanished from the pages, leaving only a name. I asked what that meant and was told the red represents the cleansing from the blood of Jesus, your Savior. Names were transferred from these books to the Lamb's Book of Life and sins were erased and remembered against you no more. The Lamb's Book of Life is for those who have received everlasting life by asking Jesus to save them. Have you? Other books were shown to me that contained prayer requests, spiritual growth in the Lord, and a record of the number of souls that one had led to Christ. The books were all very detailed, as everything we do is known to God.

John pulled a book from one of the shelves with my initials on the outside. It was the Lamb's Book of Life. He laid it open on a table and found my name recorded in the book. Next to my name were the words, "Paid in full by the precious red blood of Jesus." I praise God for what He did for me on Calvary. Because of His precious blood, I had a right to be in heaven!

We left the library, and I was taken to a grand auditorium. Everyone was clothed in glowing robes, and as I entered into the arena, I found I was clothed in a robe also. Looking up, I saw a beautiful, spiral staircase winding up loftily into the heights of the atmosphere. A beautiful, crystal clear river of water flowed directly in front of me. My eyes followed the river that flowed from the throne of God! It was an awesome sight to see the source of the river that was the throne of almighty God! Around the throne were the twenty-four elders with crowns upon their heads. A beautiful rainbow of colors encircled the throne. There were seven golden lamps with fire, signifying the presence of the Holy Spirit. John told me to drink of the water. Tasting the water, I found it to be very sweet. John then guided me into the water. Stepping in, I discovered it was only ankle deep, and then it began to rise. It covered my thighs and my shoulders, until my entire being was eventually submerged. There was no bottom, but I could easily reach down and pick up golden nuggets larger than my fist and diamonds and other precious jewels just flowed through my fingers. Jesus, The light shined upon them, producing colors that are beyond my ability to describe. The beautiful water was actually cleansing me of any debris that may have clung to me in my transition from earth to glory. In the water, John and I could communicate with one another without verbally expressing ourselves. All we needed to do was think what we wanted to say, and the other just knew what it was. Jesus was in the water playing with us and splashing it joyfully. The water receded, and we came out on the other side of the bank.

Growing along the crystal river were orchards of fruit-bearing trees. The fruit represents a gift, and when you eat the fruit, the gift explodes within you, and you become the fruit, so to speak. I'm not saying you become an apple or a pear, I mean that if the fruit you eat represents the gift of knowledge, you then have perfect understanding. I next saw the Tree of Life. The trunk of the tree was gold, and the limbs grew long and were covered with fruit. *"The Lord God planted all sorts of beautiful trees, there in the garden, trees producing the choicest fruit. At the center of the garden he placed the Tree of Life, and also the Tree of Conscience, giving knowledge of Good and Bad"* (Genesis 2:9). God created Adam and Eve and placed them in a beautiful garden, then He planted two trees. One is the Tree of Life, and the other the Tree of Death. God then gives them the choice; its life or death.

God will not force Himself on anyone. I do not blame Him. I would not want to be with someone who does not want to be with me. Think of Jesus as that Tree of Life—you can choose Him and live forever. Think of Satan as the Tree of Death—you can choose him and have eternal death forever. Adam and Eve chose the wrong tree. Which tree do you choose? *"To him that overcometh will I give to eat the tree of life, which is in the midst of the paradise of God"* (Revelation 2:7 KJV). First John tells us, *"Whatsoever is born of God overcometh the world: and this is the victory that overcometh the world, even our faith. Who is he that overcometh the world, but he that believeth that Jesus is the Son of God?"* (1 John 5:4–5 KJV) The only way to become an overcomer is by putting your faith in Jesus.

Then I saw a multitude of people, all singing: "All hail the power of Jesus' name, let angels prostrate fall." They were from every tribe, nationality, and every color upon the face of the earth. I asked John why they were singing a song from the Baptist hymnal in heaven, and he replied, "Gary, all songs of the Spirit originate here in heaven, then they are given to someone on earth who will then birth that song into existence." It would be many years later that I would hear songs that I had first heard in heaven being sung here on earth, songs like "Alleluia" and "He Is Lord." There is something else I learned about the music. Many of the songs we hear in the secular world were stolen from heaven. Think about what I am about to say carefully, and see if it doesn't make perfect sense. We know from the writings in Ezekiel that Satan was in charge of the music in heaven. He was the director of music. When Satan was cast out of heaven, he took songs that were intended to be songs of praise for our Lord Jesus and perverted the words, counterfeited them, and gave them to the world. That is why, when you hear a song on a Christian radio station today that was a popular "rock" song years ago, it is not because the Christian musician has stolen it from the world, it is simply because the Holy Spirit has put it back into its original form.

The hills and mountains before us towered in breathtaking beauty. I noticed a host of people on the hillside. They were observing things that were taking place on earth. When they witnessed a lost soul being told about the saving grace of God, if that person accepted Jesus as his Lord and Savior, all the people on the hillsides, mountain tops, and in the city would break out in applause and spontaneous praise. The mountains would begin to sing and the trees in heaven would clap their limbs together. And you could hear, "Rejoice, rejoice, for a lost soul is coming home!" *"For ye shall go out with joy and be led forth with peace: the mountains and the hills shall break forth before you into singing, and all the trees of the field shall clap with their hands"* (Isaiah 55:12 KJV). Isn't it wonderful to know that when you tell someone about Jesus, you have all of heaven cheering you on? Hebrews twelve tells us about this great host of witnesses. I saw a man come to Christ and these witnesses went and found his mother to tell her that her son had accepted Jesus.

John then took me by what looked to be a school-area playground, with golden fountains and marble benches. Flowers grew everywhere, producing a fragrance like sweet-smelling perfume. I marveled at the brilliant colors that the flowers had, each one was different from the other flowers, and no two were alike, not like here on earth, where if you've seen one daisy, you've seen them all. I marveled in amazement with the sheer delight that I experienced when I heard a sweet melody of praise being sung by the flowers! They were so vivid and so alive that I could actually see expression in each one. The flowers were singing. I saw a tiny little girl with long, brown hair that hung in ringlets down her back. She wore a white robe that glistened in the light of our Lord. She had sandals on her small feet. When she saw Jesus, she began to run towards him with her arms stretched out. Jesus stooped down and caught her as she leapt into his arms. Then from all directions children came running to see Jesus. There were children of every race and color. They all wore robes of white and sandals. They sat at His feet and listened intently as He ministered to them. I will never forget the way their tiny faces glowed with rapture as they looked up at Jesus. "Jesus Loves All the Children of the World." While Jesus was ministering to them, all sorts of animals were with the children. It was an awesome sight to see a magnificent lion frolicking with the children, as if it were a kitten, and seeing birds of elegant beauty sitting on shoulders and tops of heads. I saw teenagers that had left this earth prematurely. They were playing in crystal pools of water, laughing and singing. People in heaven are always joyfully dancing and singing praises to celebrate Jesus. I have been in many churches that could have been mistaken for a funeral service instead of rejoicing in the Lord Jesus Christ. They act like their best friend had just died. There are a lot of people who are going to have to go to school in heaven to learn how to praise God! I wanted to go and talk to Jesus. John said, "You will, but first come see the other things I have to show you."

As John and I walked the transparent gold streets of the city, I saw the brilliance of Jesus the Son shining on it. The soft colors of light seemed to come alive with glitter in a ballet of color, gracefully dancing on those streets of gold. The streets are crystal clear, yet they are pure gold. I had an atheist approach me not too long ago who told me if I was going to go around making up silly stories about heaven that I needed to get my facts straight, and that any fool knew that gold was yellow and not transparent. It is a proven fact that there is an impurity in gold that makes it yellow. Nothing in heaven is impure.

Someone else once said to me that they believed heaven was just a "state." My response was, "Like Texas?" There is a country song that says, "If Heaven's Not like Texas, I Don't Want to Go." Well, I can tell you folks that it is not! Praise God it's not! It seems so strange to me that so many people relate to heaven as just a place where we're going to be floating around on a cloud, strumming a harp and looking down on the earth. That's so far from the truth. There will be many new adventures for us as we do what God asks us to do. There is more life in heaven than there will ever be here on earth. Even the flowers sing praises to Jesus and rejoice in His wonderful name!

I saw angels carrying golden bowls filled with a liquid substance. I asked John what it was, and he told me it was the tears of the saints below. Every time a child of God prays so earnestly that a tear drop falls, an angel is there to catch that tear and deliver it to God. The tears are stored in golden bowls at the base of God's throne. I saw other angels carrying golden vials filled with a vapor-like substance. I asked the angels what it was, and they replied, "It is the praises of the people on earth presented to God as sweet smelling incense." When we praise God, angels collect that praise and take it directly to God.

I saw so many angels. All magnificent in beauty, some had wings, while others did not. They each had their own personality and identity. Each angel had a great countenance. God has given them a great intelligence. The word *angel* means "messenger." Angels are God's messengers. Many people believe that angels were once men and women and upon dying, were transformed into angelic beings. Nowhere in the Bible does it mention this. Jesus created them as angels. There were no lazy angels! Each angel was working diligently at whatever task he was assigned. All were joyfully serving God. I have heard many untrue ideas about angels lately, such as they are cute, fat, little rosy-cheeked cupid dolls, who flutter around bringing happy, good feelings, and they are available to anyone at any one time. *"No, for the angels are only spirit messengers sent out to help and care for those who are to receive his salvation"* (Hebrews 1:14). Angels are not sent out to help those who have rejected Christ. New Age people say that you can contact your angels whenever you need help with your love life, finances, for protection, or simply because you are lonesome and need your angel for company. They also say you can contact your angel by channeling or wearing the right colors or it may even be as simple as writing a letter to your angel. Oh, brother! To seek out angels, looking for anything of the spirit other than a close walk with the Lord, is welcoming demon activity with open arms and is very dangerous. Peace and comfort can only come from the Holy Spirit, and we are never to invoke aid by calling on angels to render their assistance in times of need. We are to call only on God. It is God who sends the angels to assist us; they act only under His direction and never apart from Him. We should be very thankful to God that He has given us the protection of His holy angels during our earthly pilgrimage. Angels are under subjection to God. They are, however, free like us to make their own choices. (Free but within the limits of God's laws.) We are to keep our eyes on Jesus Christ! There are angels which have fallen from God's grace, because they have acted independently of God. Satan and his demons were once holy angels. *"You were on the holy mount of God; you walked among the fiery stones. You were blameless in your ways from the day you were created till wickedness was found in you"* (Ezekiel 28:14–15 NIV). The devil is not a myth. He's not the cute, little, red guy on your deviled ham. He does not have pointed ears, horns growing from his head, and a pitchfork. Because he has been pictured this way, some people claim that Satan is not a real being—that he is Greek mythology and does not exist. No doubt this idea was inspired by Satan himself. After all, if there is no devil then there is no hell, therefore no reason to receive Jesus as Savior. What would be the point? If there is nothing to be saved from, why did was it that "God so *loved the world that He gave His only begotten Son....That the world through Him might be saved"* (John 3:16–17 NKJV). The Bible teaches us of the reality of Satan's existence as certainly as the existence of God. *"You were the seal of perfection, full of wisdom and perfect in beauty"* (Ezekiel 28:11 NKJV). Satan was created perfect in beauty. Today, Satan uses his beauty to lead many astray. I was in a local bookstore not too long ago, and I picked up a best-selling book, written about a lady's after death experience. She wrote that you don't need Jesus' salvation, because no one goes to hell, because there is no hell. My heart broke because Satan has used his power and beauty to deceive her. The untruths that she wrote are now a best-selling book that has led countless others away from the truth of Jesus Christ. As I stood there looking over the shelves, I counted eight other books about after death experiences. All eight of them have "The Light" in the title. I heard the Holy Spirit tell me "the name 'Lucifer' means light bearer." Second Corinthians 11:14 tells us that Satan comes transformed as an angel of light. He is very beautiful, yet he is a very dangerous and deceptive light. Satan is real! He hates God and his purpose is to steal us from Him. People are being blinded by the light rather than being embraced by it.

We entered into a room that was like a nursery. I saw what looked like big globs of flesh, heaped into mounds. That's the only way I know how to describe it—just big globs of flesh that looked like mounds of clay. There was an angel with each one. "What is that?" I asked. John replied, "That is aborted babies from the earth below. An angel has been assigned to each one who will fashion and form them into the child God intended them to be." Keep in mind that this happened in 1966. There were no statistics kept on the number of abortions performed during that time. Statistics now show that 1.5 million to 2 million babies are being aborted every year in America alone.

Sometimes the Lord will make a face stand out in the crowd, telling me to go pray for them. At one service, a young woman stood in the back of the church, her face stood out to me, and I went to her. She hesitated when I asked her if I could pray for her, and then she said, "Go ahead, I guess it couldn't hurt." I laid my hands on her shoulders and the Holy Spirit spoke through me saying, "Father, bless this woman and the baby in her womb." The girl's eyes got as big as saucers and she backed backwards saying, "Don't pray that." The Holy Spirit rose up inside me and I said, "I know what I'm doing." I bound up the evil spirit that was harassing her, and she fell under the power of the Holy Spirit. I led her to the Lord. She then told me that for the past year she had been having an affair with a married man and as a result had become pregnant. Nobody knew that she was pregnant, except God who knows all things. She had an appointment at 9:00 the next morning to get an abortion, but she changed her mind and now knew that she would have the child. Seven and a half months later, my wife and I received a birth announcement—It's a Girl! That baby girl was almost cast away before her time. Jesus cares deeply about the aborted lives; the unwanted children of the earth. He also cares for the mothers who do not see any other alternative. They do not know that God is able to give strength in times of trouble. He is tender and forgiving. God is so good! If you have had an abortion, or are a man who has talked your wife, girlfriend, or maybe even your daughter into having an abortion, God will forgive all your sins, even the ones you have yet to forgive yourself for. Ask for His forgiveness and everlasting mercy.

Nowadays, many women and men think nothing of destroying their unborn babies, because a child may be inconvenient. The value of life has been so cheapened by abortion. It's a sorrowful thought to me that God may have had to move the unborn to a larger room. They are not a fetus, they are a real person known to God, and He values everyone.

After we left the nursery, we walked into a long building, much like a storage building. I was caught off guard by what I saw hanging from the walls. There were rows of legs, rows of arms, cubicles with hair and eyeballs of various colors. Every part of one's anatomy was in this room. You might be wondering why does there need to be a place like this in heaven? It reminds me of the joke, "Were you out of the room when God was passing out brains?" John knew that I didn't understand, and he told me to watch what happens. Before my eyes, from my heavenly vantage point, I could see the prayers of the saints below shooting up like arrows towards heaven. Angels would receive the prayers and bring them into the throne room of God. God would grant the prayer request, and the angel would be dispatched from that room to deliver the miracle. If a doctor says that something is no good and must be removed, I'm telling you that God has a miracle for you. God has a spare parts room! You say, "Well, I know people who needed a miracle, they may have even asked for one, and did not receive it." Let me tell you what I saw next. I saw the angels dispatched with the answered miracle from God, fighting principalities and powers, only to be stopped by doubt and unbelief from the mouth of the petitioner.

Such things as "It's not for me," or "It's not God's will that I be healed" is what I heard them say. Then the angel would sadly turn around and take the miracle back to heaven and deposit it into a room called unclaimed blessings. I have read the New Testament over and over and have not once found where Jesus turned anyone away saying, "No, it is not my will that you be healed." Most of us believe in the doctor more that we believe in Jesus' power to heal us. I tell you why I believe this. The news media tells us when to get sick. It is "cold and hay fever season." Commercials on TV begin promoting their cure, we get the symptoms, and begin to take cold remedies or go to the doctor. You may think I'm anti-doctor, but I'm not. I'm just simply trying to wake up God's people to the fact that there is a better way to live.

> One day in a certain village he was visiting, there was a man with an advanced case of leprosy. When he saw Jesus, he fell to the ground before him, face downward in the dust, begging to be healed. "Sir," he said, "if you only will, you can clear me of every trace of my disease." Jesus reached out and touched the man and said, "Of course I will. Be healed." And the leprosy left him instantly. (Luke 5:12–13)

If you are in need of a miracle from God, don't stop asking. Grab hold of the horns of the altar of God and refuse to let go until the miracle power of God is manifested in your behalf. Faith does not just believe God can, faith believes God will. Stop speaking doubt and unbelief and start speaking faith! There are people who make things happen, and there are people who ask "what happened?" *"Anything is possible if you have faith"* (Mark 9:23). What is faith? *"Faith is the substance of things hoped for, the evidence of things not seen"* (Hebrews 11:1 KJV).

> *Surely he hath borne our griefs, and carried our sorrows: yet, we did esteem him stricken of God and afflicted. He was wounded for our transgressions, he was bruised for our iniquities: the chastisement of our peace was upon him; and by his stripes we are healed.* (Isaiah 53:4–5)

God the Father so willed our healing that He sent His only Son to suffer so that we don't have to. This scripture leaves no room for doubt; that by His stripes we are healed! Claim your blessing so it won't be put back in the room of unclaimed blessings. The Bible tells us that Jesus is the same yesterday, today, and forever. He healed the sick when He walked this earth, and He still heals today!

John then led me through gates that sparkled of precious stones. Up the walkway stood the mansion where I will spend all eternity. It had great, marble columns, like some of the plantations you see in the South. It was magnificent. Walking into the mansion, we entered into what would be like a living room area. There was no furniture, only three buckets of paint sitting there. I had seen other mansions that had furniture, art on the walls, some even had pets—all the trappings of suburbia that we have here on earth.

No two mansions were alike, God knows you better than you know yourself. He knows your hearts desires, your likes and dislikes. If you have called on Jesus to save you, your custom-designed mansion in paradise is under construction, being made perfect for your liking.

John walked over and dipped his hand into one of the buckets and flung it against the wall, and instantly, a beautiful floral arrangement appeared. "This place needs more decorating," he said, handing me a bucket. If you really got to know me, you would find my nature to be exuberant, so I took the entire bucket and flung it against the wall. Suddenly, there was this beautiful, floral garden and scenery that was manifested before my eyes. A beautiful fragrance, like roses, consumed the room. I stood there gazing at the splendor of it all, thinking, *Could this be all for me? Could the answer be as simple as "Yes, because Jesus loves me"?* John looked at me and said, "It's not ready for occupancy just yet, so you need to leave." Jesus says, "*In my Father's house are many mansions*" (John 14:2 NKJV). I know this to be true, I have seen mine.

"*Christ was alive when the world began, yet I myself have seen him with my own eyes and listened to him speak. I have touched him with my own hands. He is God's message of life*" (1 John 1:1). I could not have said it better than what the disciple John wrote.

I have never seen anyone or anything that could possibly compare to the beauty of our Lord Jesus, who I now stood before. Even though there are no words to express His divine presence, I will, to the best of my ability, try to describe to you what I felt as I talked to Jesus. He looked at me with the bluest eyes I have ever seen. I fell before Him like I was a dead man at His feet, which shone as fine, polished brass. He reached a nail scarred hand out to me and lifted me up, praise God! That is the business Jesus is in—picking you up and putting you back on your feet again! He then lifted me into His arms and held me to His chest as if I were a little child. I felt the most wonderful, joyful, peaceful, powerful love I have ever felt.

I have been writing about the glories and beauty of heaven, but we must never lose sight of the Lord Jesus. For all is given that you might know, love, and serve Jesus. He is the real subject of this book. Because we ask, Lord, what will we see in heaven? "I will be your focus." What will we hear in heaven? "Worship and enjoy me forever." What will we know in heaven? "All that I reveal to you." What is heaven? "It is my creation for you. Jesus is the center of it all!"

His hair and beard are as white as snow. He wears a regal robe of righteousness with a beautiful, purple sash that says *"King of Kings and Lord of Lords"* (Revelation 19:16), with a belt of solid gold around His waist. I saw indentions etched across His brow and forehead from the crown of thorns that had been placed on His head on that fateful day at Calvary. He is the *"Alpha and Omega, the beginning and the end"* (Revelation 22:13 KJV). His name is *"Wonderful…The Prince of Peace"* (Isaiah 9:6 KJV). He is *"the Lamb of God, which taketh away the sin of the world"* (John 1:29 KJV). He is called *"a friend that sticketh closer than a brother"* (Proverbs 18:24 KJV). He is the Lord of Glory! Which *"none of the princes of the world knew: for if they had known it, they would not have crucified the Lord of glory,"* (1 Corinthians 2:8 KJV). Oh, what glory awaits those of us who know Jesus! None can compare to Him! No words can do Him justice! I want to spend a thousand years just sitting at His feet. I want to look into those compassionate eyes and worship Him through all eternity! I will never be content until I once again see His wonderful face! He wore a prayer shawl, for He is Jewish.

Jesus spoke to me, and just as God almighty wrote the Ten Commandments with the tip of His finger, He wrote these words on my heart. He told me "there was a song for me to sing, a missionary journey I am to take, a book for me to write, and that there was a purpose for me being here in this life." Then Jesus looked right at me with those piercing blue eyes and said, "Don't ever buy the condemnation of the devil that you are unworthy. You are worthy. You have been redeemed by the Blood of the Lamb." He said, "Why do my people not believe in me? Why do my people reject me? Why do they not walk in my commandments?" Jesus commissioned me to make Him real to the people of this earth. He said that there would be three things that would mark His soon return: a Spirit of restoration, a Spirit of prayer, and an outburst of miracles.

A Spirit of Restoration

Jesus told me, "Remember what I say, for the Father and I are one. When I speak, the Father has spoken. Above all else love one another and always be forgiving towards each other."

He said that the Spirit of restoration will prevail throughout the land. Has there ever been a time in history that we need the Lord to send a spirit of restoration more than now? Marriages are falling apart faster than ever. People want to leave out the words *commitment, obey,* and *'til death do us part* in most marriage ceremonies. Lifelong friends are conveniently forgetting the loyal characteristics of a friendship. Children are taking their parents to divorce court. Parents are relinquishing most of the responsibility of their children. Neighbors are killing one another over mailboxes, and churches are full of back-biting, gossiping whispers. *"And because iniquity shall abound, the love of many shall wax cold"* (Matthew 24:12 KJV). People hold on to hurt feelings and hold grudges, and it seems that when forgiveness is asked for, the wounded party is unable to forgive. Compassion and forgiveness have become only words. Love waxes cold because of the iniquity in the heart. If the heart is full of the love of Jesus, then one is able to overlook rejection and hurt and is able to love those who hurt them. Jesus can restore our abilities to forgive. *"If someone says, 'I love God,' and hates his brother, he is a liar; for he who does not love his brother whom he has seen, how can he love God whom he has not seen?"* (1 John 4:20 NKJV). Because of my love for God, I can feel an abundance of love for my brothers and sisters, even those who hate me and speak evil against me. It is only through Jesus that I can do this. From a human standpoint, this is not always easily accomplished. That is when I have to ask the Lord to fill my heart with love for them, so I will not show hate, envy, or bitterness.

God is going to start sending people in your pathway. People who have offended you, people you may have offended. You are going to have to make a choice: either make amends, forgiveness is a must if you want to walk in the fullness of God, or you can let bitterness and anger defeat you.

In my own life, God dealt some really heavy truths to me about forgiveness towards my parents. I had been trying to forget instead of forgive. There is a big difference. To forget is just a way of covering up pain. To forgive is to let go of the pain. As I said earlier, I was physically and emotionally abused by both my mother and father. My father sexually abused me, and I still have scars on the insides of my legs where he put his cigarettes out on me. Those scars will never go away. But the scars on my heart have been removed through the love of Jesus. When Jesus taught us the Lord's Prayer, He tells us to pray for forgiveness as we forgive one another. In the verse following the Lord's Prayer, He tells us that our forgiveness is subject to our forgiving. *"Your heavenly Father will forgive you if you forgive those who sin against you; but if you refuse to forgive them, he will not forgive you"* (Matthew 6:14–15). There are Christians who are in danger of losing their forgiveness from God because of their inability to forgive others. This is serious! You must realize that there is no place in heaven for those who are unforgiving, unloving, mean, rude, or unkind. Never gossip or be jealous. *"Instead, be kind to each other, tenderhearted, forgiving one another, just as God has forgiven you because you belong to Christ"* (Ephesians 4:32). In one of my recent sermons, a man asked me to pray with him, because for the past seven years he had no communication with his parents. Hardly a week had passed when a couple stood in front of me. They received Jesus Christ as their Lord and Savior, and with tears streaming down their faces, they said, "Would you please pray that our son will come home?" I looked up and saw that the same young man who had asked me to pray with him earlier was standing behind this couple. "Mama, Dad, I am here," he said. They fell into each other's arms in one big, group hug. That hug included me. His father kept saying, "That is the fastest prayer I've ever seen answered." I truly believe the Spirit of Restoration is upon us now.

Speech Language Pathologist's Report: Gary Wood's Ability to Speak Without a Larynx

Recently, when Gary was holding Camp meeting in Mechanicsville, Virginia, a speech pathologist spoke to him about the details of his miracle. It blessed Gary so much that he had her share with the church body. This is her observation of his miracle.

My name is Rashida. I've been really excited about camp meeting, because this week I got the flier, and it gave the description about Evangelist Gary Wood. I was like, *"what?"* I was just so amazed about his voice and the larynx. As a speech language pathologist, I deal with the voice also. That's why I had a big interest in it. I said to Mrs. Winfree, who is an elder in our church, "I don't think that people realize that this is really a miracle."

I talked to Brother Wood Monday night, and I said, "Brother Wood, I have to share something with you."

He said, "Okay, honey, what is it?"

I said "You know, today I went in the basement in the archives and got out my voice book from college, because there has to be more that the larynx is used for than just talking." For those of you who don't know, he was in a horrible accident and his whole larynx got crushed. When I looked in my book, it said that there were three functions of the larynx.

First of the functions is for biological purposes. That means that it protects the airway. When you eat food and liquids, which as you know, they are supposed to go into your stomach. If you don't have your larynx, it dumps into your lungs and you get pneumonia and die. I thought, well, that's amazing, his larynx was crushed.

Second is an emotional function, which means that he's able to show whether he's happy or sad when we listen to his voice. That's amazing! His larynx was crushed.

Third was a linguistic function. That means that his voice is able to get loud, soft, you know, things like that. He can holler and scream. I said, "That's amazing!"

Then I talked to one of my friends, Shay, who is also a speech therapist. I told her about it, and she dropped the phone in unbelief. She said, "Well, Rashida, you have to remind him that science has not yet found a way to give him a transplant." You can get a heart transplant, but you cannot get a larynx transplant. You can get a knee replacement, but you can't get your larynx replaced. It's so small and intricate that they haven't been able to do that. I was thinking this is unbelievable! I told him that it is wonderful that he is here talking, but all of my speech friends wanted to know how his voice sounded.

"Well, is it, you know, weak?"

"No", I said. "He sounds normal". They thought he had a speech therapist work with him, and that's how he was able to talk. But, you see, we only teach you two types of speech. Esophageal speech, which is a kind of like a burp. The other is where we give you an electronic device, which is like an artificial larynx. You put it right here at your stoma. You've seen people with those little microphones. I was amazed, he doesn't have those things. My speech friends could not believe it. I said seriously, he talks like normal everyday people.

When Gary Wood asked me to tell you all this information, I'm thinking to myself, *Lord, he had this accident in 1966, and he gets all the way to Richmond, Virginia, for me to tell him this information. I wasn't even born in 1966!* I was doubting the field I should be in. I hear people who just love what they do. I'm like, it's all right being a speech therapist, but I don't love it like that! So when I shared this information with Bro Gary about something that happened over thirty-five years ago, I thought, *Well, maybe this is supposed to be my profession.*

One other thing I want to share is that if your larynx is not there or if you had a laryngectomy, you cannot lift even a book, or you wouldn't be able to move the lectern down, because you need the larynx to give you breath for support. I was like, *This is deep! I mean this man is doing all of these things that he's not even supposed to be doing.*

When I was listening to him, I kept thinking, *when I hear him sing "There's Power in the Blood," I think, praise God, you are right, Gary Wood. You are washed in the blood because what you just did is a medical miracle.*

This testimony was given at Lighthouse Christian Center, in Mechanicsville, a suburb of Richmond, Virginia. Phone number: 804-730-0101.

A Spirit of Prayer

While I was with Jesus, He showed me the earth. It was like I was looking at the pictures the astronauts send to us on earth from the satellite; only the earth was encircled by three rings. Inside the first ring, the earth's atmosphere, I saw hundreds of evil spirits. This is Satan's domain. The evil spirits would target people and try to deceive them. If the people would accept the lies as truth, many more demons would swarm in like flies. They would then begin to fall to the temptations of the flesh by allowing the demons to control them, and their lives would begin to fall apart. The demons have power to make people tell lies, cheat, steal, commit adultery, and speak evil against one another. It was like the people became puppets on a string.

Then Jesus showed me that when a child of God got down on their knees before Him, praying in the name of Jesus, with faith, their prayers would shoot into the heavens like barbed arrows. An army of angelic forces would appear, prepared for battle to destroy the demons' effectiveness. The more prayers of faith there were, the more the demons would retreat. But if doubt and unbelief were spoken, the demons would begin to overcome.

The Lord told me that as time grows closer to His return, demon activity will become more rampant. Satan knows that the final curtain is being drawn, and his time is running out. Millions of demons and their satanic powers abound all around us. Why are we so besieged by demonic powers? It is because we pray so little. The results are immorality, perversion, child abuse, poverty, abortion, wars, revolutions, pornography, the occult, an increase in crime, and sicknesses such as HIV/AIDS, just to name a few. *"Put on the whole armour of God, that ye may be able to stand against the wiles of the devil. For we wrestle not against flesh and blood, but against principalities, against powers, against the rulers of the darkness of this world, against spiritual wickedness in high places"* (Ephesians 6:11–12 KJV). Put on your armor and take a stand against the workings of the devil. You can only arm yourself with the *Word of God*. If you do not read or study the Bible, you have no defense against the forces of darkness that are always at work to defeat you. With faith, tear down the strongholds of the devil and surrender your life to the Holy Spirit. I have come to believe that, beyond a shadow of a doubt, the greatest need of mankind is prayer. Our only hope to destroy the demonic powers in the world today is through the *Spirit of Prayer*.

Miracles

The third thing Jesus told me is there will be a supernatural release of miracles. I've witnessed blind eyes opened, crippled people have thrown down their crutches and leapt out of their wheelchairs and begin walking. People with no hope for recovery of cancer, diabetes, and HIV/AIDS have been healed. I have seen the multiplication of food and money. I have seen the dead come back to life.

By now, you may have wondered, *My word, how long was this guy dead? For him to have seen and done so much in heaven, Rigor mortis has most likely set in.*

You and I operate in a realm called *time*. We live our lives according to time. "I've got to go to work at 8:30 A.M.. I've got an appointment at 2:00 P.M." God is not limited by time. He operates in the realm called *eternity*. I was asked to teach a mid-week Bible study in a couples' home that I had never met before. Near the end of the evening the Holy Spirit began to minister to me saying that someone was there who was having chest pains and they had been having pain all day. I asked that whoever it was to let me pray with them. Nobody came forward. Going home, we had been driving for about fifteen minutes when one of the ladies said, "Oh, Gary, I left my purse back at their house." There were six of us in the car. After I turned around, I looked at the clock and commented that it was 10:30. I went up to the door, and the lady of the house grabbed me by the arm, pulling me in and saying, "Oh, thank God, you came back! It's my husband! He's at the table. It's his heart!" He was slumped over the kitchen table, and he was blue. I laid hands on him and began to pray. I asked Jesus to put life back into his lifeless body. When all of a sudden, I felt a charge of electricity surge through me! Every hair on my body stood on end, and I was thrown backwards into the wall! All my strength was drained and I just slid down the wall. You see, we can't handle the full power of God, that's why we fall in His presence. All at once, that dead man sat straight up.

And his color returned to normal. His wife said, "Oh honey, I thought you were gone!"

He said, "I was, I've been in heaven, and I saw Jesus. Jesus told me that He was sending Gary to pray for me, and that I would be healed." He had had two previous heart attacks. When he went to his doctor for an examination, the EKG confirmed that his heart was completely healed. There were no signs of him ever having a bad heart. God gave him a new heart.

After all this excitement, a good hour had elapsed. Driving home again, the three of us in the front seat looked at the clock and exclaimed, "It's 10:30." God will stop time for you!

A few years ago on Halloween a man saw a newspaper article that read "Man Raised from the Dead." He told his son "Let's not go trick or treating. Let's go to this meeting to see the dead man, it will be a blast. We can have a lot of fun."

So they came to the meeting wearing masks that looked like monsters and sat on the front row. All during the service the father poked his son, mocked me, and snickered while I gave my testimony. At the end of the service the Spirit of God took over and convicted that man. He took off his mask and as he came forward, he was crying when he said, "I'm an alcoholic and I lost my wife. I want to give my life to God tonight." His son had followed him to the altar and he also received Jesus as his personal Lord and Savior.

Since I've been in the ministry under the leading of the Holy Spirit, I have seen God's kindness and grace for His people. But the most wonderful and the most merciful of all His mighty miracles is salvation!

Testimony of Ricardo A. Perez
I Was Saved By the Grace of God on 11/29/2000

I was saved by the grace of God on November 29, 2000. My family often spoke to me about Jesus, but I wouldn't listen. After going to a Promise Keepers meeting of 22,000 men, I was touched by God, but I stopped searching and lost the joy I found there in the meeting.

My wife was scheduled for surgery, and we both wound up in the hospital. I broke my ankle in three places and was also hospitalized five days. God spoke to me about my need for Him at that time. Later that week I was invited to Agape Worship Center to hear evangelist Gary Wood preach. I began to cry as I came into the church. They were playing my favorite song. I knew something was going to happen to me that night.

Brother Wood began to preach about the river of God and invited all to come to the altar and drink. I found myself standing in front of him as he asked, "do you want a drink?"

I said, "Yes." And began to cry and shake—I felt like a new person. I was cleansed of sin and started a new beginning. My crutches fell to the floor, and my ankle was healed from that moment on.

Now, it is nine months later, and I am a member of Agape Worship Center. I have made this my home, and I will worship the Lord always. I have a vital relationship with Jesus and bring family and friends to church so they also can begin a relationship with Jesus.

Thanks, Brother Gary Wood, for the words of encouragement.

—Ricardo Perez, August 2001
Agape Worship Center, Bloomfield, New Jersey

The following is a testimony told by Terance Hopkins of Lufkin, Texas

I grew up in church, cut my first tooth on the back of a pew. I called Jesus, Lord, and believed that He died for my sins. I was baptized in water and with the Holy Spirit. I was saved at an early age. As I grew older, the temptations of the world drew me away from Jesus. I left Him for life on the wild side. Wine, women, and song—that was the path for me. Jesus never leaves us, but we sure can leave Him. I never saw the train, until it was too late. My truck was torn in two and my head was crushed. I was killed instantly. My spirit left my body, and I was in a very bright tunnel that engulfed my being with such perfect peace. I could hear angels singing. It was beautiful. I stood on a hill that over-looked a city, it sparkled of solid gold. It was a spectacular sight! A sweet and wonderful feeling came over me.

The next thing I knew, I was standing in the very presence of Jesus. His power and glory was more than I could stand, so I fell to the ground like a dead man. He lifted me up and said, "My son, I have work for you to do. If you do not wish to do the work that I have for you, then let me show you where you will be going with the way you have been living in the past." As far as I could see, were pits of fire. It was so big, like a canyon with high, rocky walls. I saw thousands of people in hell. They were constantly burning but not being consumed. Some people think that if you go to hell, that you just burn up and cease to exist. Your soul lives forever. If you go to hell, you will be in eternal torment and suffering forever. Some were trying to climb the walls. I saw one man climbing; I could see from the way the walls were formed that there was no escaping hell. A demon spirit flew up and knocked him back into the fire. Other demons began to hit and beat him with clubs that had long spikes on the ends. Pain-filled screams and mournful cries filled the air. I was gripped with fear and began to shake uncontrollably.

Demons began to torment me saying, "You could have had Jesus! You could have had heaven!" I knew that what they were saying was true. I was just in heaven, and it was so beautiful. I had felt such joy. I wished I had been faithful to Jesus so that I could have stayed in heaven. If only I had repented before it was too late. I began to cry with great sobs, gasping and pleading with Jesus to take me away from there. I was in spirit form, and I was crying. I had all my senses. They had become even more sensitive. I have never been so aware of sorrow, grief, and eternal death as I was in hell! I knew that all the people in hell could feel all these things too. I never, in my worst nightmares, dreamed that hell could have possibly been this horrible. It is a place of sorrow beyond your belief! I could hear piercing screams and groaning sounds. If you have never asked Jesus into your heart to save you, *do it today!* If you have left Jesus and have backslidden, repent and ask Him to forgive you. Please, don't put it off!

I looked at Jesus and saw great sorrow on His face; tears were falling down His cheeks. I felt my spirit being pulled, and I was back in my body. My aunt had called a preacher that she knew, Gary Wood. He came up to the hospital at once. About the time that he got there, I had died again. I remember my spirit leaving my body. I could see the doctors and nurses working to keep me alive. A nurse was shaking her head because my condition was hopeless. My doctor went to tell my parents, *"I'm sorry, there's nothing that I can do."* That's when Gary spoke up.

"There's something that I can do." He was wearing a bright pink Hawaiian shirt, Bermuda shorts, flip-flops, and a gold chain around his neck. My mother was wondering who in the world this character was? She thought, *God does not listen to people who wear jewelry and shorts.*

But Momma was in a state of despair and said, "Go on in there, what harm can it do?" Gary came in, laid hands on me, and began to pray, calling on the mighty name of Jesus! My spirit once again entered into my body. From that point on, Gary stayed by my side. I died three more times, and Gary was there to pray for me. The doctors told my parents that the only reason I'm alive is because of God. I thank God for Gary! If it wasn't for his faith in Jesus; I know where I'd be right now! *I want no part of that place called hell!*

I want to assure you that the things written in this book are true. Heaven is a real place of beauty and everlasting joy. It can be your home if you have accepted Jesus as your Savior. I also must warn you that hell is equally as real. It is a place of eternal doom and damnation. If you have never asked Jesus to save you, or if you are a back-slider, please take time right now to kneel and ask Jesus to forgive you of your sins. It's not just by "chance" that you are reading this book.

—Terance Hopkins
Lufkin, Texax

"So, Jesus promised to come back, did he? Then where is He? He'll never come! Why, as far back as anyone can remember, everything has remained exactly as it was since the first day of creation."

Have you ever heard anyone say this almost word for word, maybe you yourself have scoffed at the second coming of Jesus in such a way.

"First, I want to remind you that in the last days there will come scoffers who will do every wrong they can think of and laugh at the truth" (2 Peter 3:3). So, even those that scoff are fulfilling the prophecy of these last days. Yes, Jesus is coming back. He himself promised time and time again that He would return. The second coming is mentioned three hundred and eighteen times in the New Testament. In the Old Testament there are twenty times as many prophecies about the second coming than there are about the first.

Before I left heaven, I saw the most beautiful golden trumpet. It was on a stand of gold that glistened with diamonds and jade. One day soon, God is going to call Jesus to Him and say, "Son, it is time to call the children home." And the archangel will blow that golden trumpet with a mighty blast, and in the twinkling of an eye, all of us who love Jesus and eagerly await His return will be caught up to meet Him in the clouds. I believe this catching up—the rapture—will take place soon. In fact, I am so sure of this, that if I die again, I'll be surprised! I must warn you that if you do not prepare your heart in holiness and let the blood of Jesus wash you clean from all unrighteousness, you will be left behind to face the terrible fury of the tribulation. The tribulation will begin immediately following the rapture. It will be a time of terror, fear, and hopelessness such as the world has never known. You can read of the future event in Revelation 6 and 21.

Many people are deceiving themselves into thinking that they are ready. They have based their being saved on a feel good encounter with God. They had an experience with God years ago.

Because they call him Lord, they believe that they can live any way they want to, without ever having to account for themselves. They may sound religious enough; some may even seemingly fulfill the roles of the ministry.

> *Not everyone that saith unto me, Lord, Lord, shall enter into the kingdom of heaven, but he that doeth the will of my Father which is in heaven. Many will say to me in that day, Many will say to me in that day, Lord, Lord, have we not prophesied in thy name? and in thy name have cast out demons? and in thy name done many wonderful works? And then I will profess unto them, I never knew you: depart from me, ye that work iniquity.* (Matthew 7:21–23 KJV)

No, a flyby night romance with the Lord, will not keep you full of that supernatural supply of the Holy Spirit. It is a true love relationship, a daily walk with Jesus that will prepare you for that significant hour. These are the days of real heart-searching; we must give our hearts and minds completely to Him. *Are you full of the Holy Spirit?* Not, were you full. Are you full now? I know plenty of people who are full of something, and it's sure not God! God is pouring out His spirit on His sons and daughters. Many of God's people have been given dreams and visions on the soon return of the Lord Jesus Christ. These are to be taken seriously, for they are communications from God.

A friend of mine was given this dream:

Before my eyes was a huge tree, like an oak. The leaves of the tree shimmered and sparkled in the sunlight as they rustled in the breeze. Fruit began to grow. At first one or two peach-like fruits appeared. Then, there were many, until the limbs were completely covered, and I could not see a single leaf. Then a hand appeared and began to pick the fruit. As the hand harvested the fruit, each piece was rolled over in the palms, being inspected for the quality.

Much the same as we do at the market, not wanting to accept any that is not good enough. If the fruit was good and without blemish then it was placed in a basket. I saw fruit that appeared perfect on one side, but as the hand rolled the fruit to the other side, it was rotten to the core. That piece of fruit was disregarded and thrown to the side. The Lord woke me from my dream saying, "The time of my great harvest is near. I will hand-pick my chosen fruit. Only those without spot or blemish will be spared."

This sounds severe. You might say, "Then who can go?" No one is perfect. Perfection in the eyes of God comes one way and one way only, by allowing God through the Holy Spirit to correct and perfect you. *"That he might present it to himself a glorious church, not having spot, or wrinkle, or any such thing; but that it should be holy and without blemish"* (Ephesians 5:27 KJV).

> *But don't forget this, dear friends, that a day or a thousand years from now is like tomorrow to the Lord. He isn't really being slow about his promised return, even though it sometimes seems that way. But he is waiting, for the good reason that he is not willing that any should perish, and he is giving more time for sinners to repent.* (2 Peter 3:8–9)

While I am in the awesome presence of Jesus, my sister is still in the car with my body slumped over the steering wheel. Ambulances have started arriving. They have pronounced me dead at the scene of the accident. Oxygen had ceased to flow to my brain. Doctors say that without oxygen to the brain for a period of three to five minutes, if one survives, more than likely chances are one could end up brain dead, or a vegetable. I was dead for approximately twenty minutes.

My sister begins to pray and cry out, *"Oh Jesus, Jesus. He is my brother. Please, Jesus."* That name is more powerful than anything. That is the name that cancer, diabetes, and even death must bow to. That name is above every crippling disease and demonic power on the face of this earth, the name *Jesus*. The angels stand at attention, ready to be dispatched when a believer prays in faith, using the name of Jesus. "*There is salvation in no one else! Under all heaven there is no other name for men to call upon to save them*" (Acts 4:12). John looked at me and said the words that I still hear today, "You have to go back; she is using that name." I did not want to go back. I wanted to stay with Jesus. Jesus told me, "You must tell the people of the world to *get ready*, that I am coming back soon!" All eternity rolled back. I was shot out of heaven and hurled back into my body. The paramedics noticed signs of life and rushed me to San Juan County Hospital. From the impact on the steering wheel, my jaw was broken in three places, and most of my front teeth were reduced to powder and little stubs. The rest had to be extracted. You have to have a sense of humor when you've been through what I have been through. I say that my teeth are like stars, they come out at night! The turn signal indicator had broken, and the razor sharp, jagged edge crisscrossed over my face, leaving it looking like hamburger meat and did the worst damage when it sliced my vocal chords.

The impact of the steering mechanism crushed my larynx, causing my death from suffocation.

The next day, Christmas Eve 1966, I woke up in a hospital bed with my head wrapped up like a mummy. My doctors and my grandfather were standing there looking down at me. I could see that he had been crying. He told me that Sue and I had run into the back of a truck that had been illegally parked on the shoulder of the highway. My thoughts were immediately for Sue, and I wondered if she was okay. I knew she hadn't died—at least not the same time I had. "Sue is going to be fine," my grandfather said, like he had read my mind. I saw the sorrow in his eyes, and I heard the shaking in his voice when he said, "Son, you will never be able to speak again where people can understand you, let alone be able to sing." *Not sing?* I was in college on a music scholarship! Singing was my life! For the next nine months, that fact loomed like a deathly shadow over my life. *How could I tell everyone that I knew God had not sent me back for this?* Jesus had sent me back to tell people about heaven and that the only way to get there is through Him. Needless to say, I was very frustrated!

While I was having the seemingly endless, reconstructive surgeries on my face, I had plenty of time to think and pray. I thanked God for giving the doctors the ability to put me back together as well as they did. From my nose down, I had been rebuilt. I needed desperately to talk. I had to make Jesus real to the people of the world. In my desperate need, I began to read the Bible. *I needed a miracle!*

One day, while I was recuperating after surgery, I heard a song on the radio that said, "He Touched Me and Made Me Whole." I had never heard that song before. In my mind I prayed, *God, what that song says you can do. You can touch me, you can heal me, and you can make me whole like I was in heaven. I dedicate the rest of my life to tell the world about you.*

Suddenly, Jesus appeared in my room just like I had seen Him in heaven. My heart started pounding. I was filled with such awe at His beautiful presence.

Jesus had come to personally deliver my miracle! He put His gentle hand on my throat, and I felt warmth flowing through my body, especially in the area of my vocal chords. He smiled at me and was gone. He didn't come in through the door, and He didn't exit through the door. *He is the door!*

The nurse walked in and said, "Good morning, Mr. Wood. How are you doing this morning?" Why should this morning be any different? When Jesus comes into your life, something is different! You will never be the same!

I said, "Good morning."

With a startled look on her face she said, "You can't talk!"

In a booming, resounding voice I said, "Praise God, I have been healed!" Well, I just about scared her to death. She dropped my breakfast tray and went running to get the doctors. I got out of that bed and with tears of joy running down my face; I began to run around the room repeating over and over, "Praise God! Praise God! Praise God!"

Within moments, I was surrounded by doctors saying, "Open your mouth and say, ahh." They poked and prodded, and kept shaking their heads saying, "You can't do it. You should not be able to speak. You have no vocal chords. That is medically impossible." Well folks, *nothing is impossible with God.* I got a second opinion, and Doctor Jesus said *I could,* and I have been doing it ever since!

I ran down the hall and cornered a little lady in the elevator and said, "Want to hear me sing?" Picture it, I was jumping, running, and dancing all down the hallways, wearing one of those "discrete" hospital gowns! I was asking people if they wanted to hear me sing. Most of them probably thought that I had escaped from the psychiatric ward! I didn't care in the least! My God had touched me! And I know I'm healed so that I can sing it, shout it, and proclaim it from the mountain tops! That He is Lord!

After my complete recovery and discharge from the hospital, I had to take stock of my life. God had told me I had a purpose here, and He performed a creative miracle in my life that allowed me to testify to the world of His wondrous Word. I realized that I could not do this just by singing. I had to preach, so I enrolled in seminary school and became a Baptist preacher.

Ten years had passed since I had died, gone to heaven, returned to earth, and had been healed. My life was good. I had a beautiful wife and two great kids. I was one of the youngest pastors with one of the largest churches in the state. I should have been satisfied, I should have been complete. But I had a hunger, a stirring in my soul for more. It wasn't a power trip, just a thirst that wasn't being quenched. Sunday mornings I would preach and begin to cry. Weeping, I would walk around the pulpit and say, "I don't know what God wants me to do, all I know is that we are not fulfilling all that is in this Bible." I would read John 14:15–16 where Jesus would say, *"If you love me, obey me: and I will ask the Father and he will give you another Comforter, and he will never leave you."* I wasn't feeling any comfort. I wasn't sure what I was supposed to do; I just knew that I was not getting all that God had promised me. I would tell my congregation, "I don't know about you, but I want all that I have been promised by the Lord." I would just stop preaching; get down on my knees and start praying and crying. People would get up and get saved. It became very embarrassing. People were coming to church just to watch me cry! This went on for months, I had no idea what was happening to me.

One night, I received a phone call from a young man who told me that he was going to kill his wife, because she had been having an affair. The man was desperate. He was under the influence of drugs and alcohol. I went to his house and found him sitting in his car. I sat down with him and said, "You are not going to do that." This infuriated him, and the next thing I knew he had pulled a gun from his coat and was pointing it at me and pulled the trigger! I heard the deafening sound of the gun shot, and I thought I was dead again. I waited for the funnel-shaped cloud to come and get me, and then I realized that I was still alive! Against all odds the Lord protected me and I was not harmed. Sounds farfetched, I know, because the gun was at point blank range. I am not saying that I am Superman; I don't fly around in a pair of tights and leo-tards with a swirling red cape.

But, I am saying that I am God's man with a message to deliver to this world. *"We live within the shadow of the Almighty, sheltered by the God who is above all gods"* (Psalm 91:1). For the Lord says, *"Because he loves me, I will rescue him; I will make him great because he trusts in my name. When he calls on me, I will answer; I will be with him in trouble and rescue him and honor him"* (verses 14–15).

What did I do then? I grabbed the gun away from him. I don't believe in giving Satan a second chance. The man instantly sobered up and after talking with him, I was able to lead him to Christ. He and his wife worked things out, and today he is a spirit-filled preacher. *Praise God!*

I got home late that night, and you can't imagine how I was feeling. I sat in my recliner and stared at the gun as I relived the experience in my mind. That is when Deena, my wife, walked in and saw her husband, who had been crying for months, now hold-ing a revolver in his hands. She called upon the deacons of the church and told them I was freaking out. They, in turn, decided what I needed was a vacation. So they sent me off to the mountains of New Mexico, where I read the New Testament three times over. That is when I began to see that all I had been taught was not true. I had allowed my religious teachings to influence my thinking and cloud the Word of God. When you are raised Baptist, attend a Baptist Seminary, and preach the Baptist way of preaching, you only know what they teach you. The Baptists believe that when you are saved, you then receive all the Holy Spirit that you will ever receive. They do not tell you that there is a real third person of the Trinity called the Holy Spirit. It does not make any differ-ence what people think, it does not matter what you are taught in church: what matters is what God's Word says. God will not have anything to do with anything else.

I went to Dallas, Texas, to the First Annual Charismatic Conference held at the Bronco Bowl. Dr. Howard Conatser was the pastor of Beverly Hills Baptist Church. He heard my testimony, and I was asked to share with a group of about five thousand people. Near the end of the service, a lady stood up and began waving her arms around saying, "I know him! I know him! I was the nurse on duty the night of that accident! I know that what he is saying is true!" This stirred something up inside of me. That hunger was back. I went back to my hotel room and got down on my knees and began to pray. I said, "Lord Jesus, I want all the power that is available to me from heaven to earth, except speaking in tongues!" You see folks, I was a Southern Baptist preacher, and Southern Baptists do not believe in speaking in tongues. They also believe that if you do you are a devil worshipper and you run around screaming, jumping pews, and foaming at the mouth. I told God this and then began explaining our doctrine and by-laws to Him. Have you ever tried to tell God, the Creator of all, the Knower of all things, your by-laws and religious doctrine? Do you think He cares? God is not impressed with the fact that you are Southern Baptist, Methodist, Church of Christ, Lutheran, Catholic, or whatever. God either sees you as saved by His grace or not saved. I yielded to the Holy Spirit, allowing Him to baptize me, and I was hungry no more. *"For John truly baptized with water, but you shall be baptized with the Holy Spirit"* (Acts 1:5 NKJV.)

When I surrendered to the Holy Spirit, I was blessed with the gift of speaking in tongues. It changed my life, and I have now realized that it is the most precious gift, other than my salvation, that I have ever received from the Lord. People have asked me if someone needs to speak in tongues before they can go to heaven. I have told them that nowhere in the Bible does it say that. After all, I had been to heaven before I had received this gift. To receive the baptism of the Holy Spirit, all you have to do is, by faith, ask the Lord to baptize you with the Holy Spirit and He will. He is a perfect gentleman and will not force you into anything.

A friend of mine told me that she was filled with the Holy Spirit while watching Brother Benny Hinn on TV one morning. She lives in the deep East Texas woods, and cable is not available there. This was the first time she had ever seen him on TV, and has not seen him on her TV since, but this was her day to be baptized. She was getting ready for work, watching the people getting filled and healed, when Benny Hinn pointed into the TV camera and said, "You people at home, the Holy Spirit wants to fill you too." She responded by lifting her hands to the Lord. While sitting on the floor in front of the TV, she said she felt as though in slow motion, she fell back to the floor. Then coming back up to the sitting position, a most beautiful language began to flow from her lips. It was an hour drive to work from where she lives, and the language flowed the entire hour. She said she was afraid to stop, fearing she would never be able to do it again. Her tongue was numb and her mouth was dry, but this was such an awesome experience, she never wanted it to end. Once arriving at work, she knew that she would have to go back to the secular world and leave the spiritual world for a while. The first words she said in English were, "Oh Father, God, what kind of language is this?" The Lord spoke to her as she was walking across the parking lot, and said, "It is the language of the Angels."

Another lady I know was devout in her beliefs that speaking in tongues was of the devil. She had a sister who spoke in tongues and was continually giving her a hard time about it. The spirit-filled sister suggested they ask the Lord who was right. They got down on their knees and raised their faces to heaven, and my friend said, "Our Father in heaven, this speaking in tongues business— I'm right aren't I?" Before she could get another word out, she was overflowing with the beautiful, heavenly language. The baptism of the Holy Spirit is available to anyone who has been born again. I am so thankful that God's power is available to us.

I never really got to know my natural parents until after I was married and had two children of my own. I would see them from time to time, but they were like strangers for the most part. My father called me a few days before Christmas one year to tell me he was going to fly down and meet his grandchildren. Memories of my childhood came flooding into my mind. I remembered one year when he had called and asked me what I wanted for Christmas. I told him a cowboy hat, boots, and a pearl-handled, Roy Rogers cap gun, complete with quick draw holsters. Christmas came and went without so much as a phone call. This kind of thing always happened. I wouldn't hear from him until Christmas, and then I got empty promises. I was afraid of this happening again, but I told him to come, not expecting him to show. This time was different. He was different. When I answered the door to find him dressed in a Santa Claus suit with a sack full of presents, I was taken by surprise, to say the least. He was trying to make up for all the Christmases that he had missed. Before he left us to go home, he told me that he had heard me preach on a tape and had asked Jesus to save him. Not long after that, I received a phone call learning he had died from lung cancer. His doctor said he could have died on the plane trip and that while he was in the hospital he would play my tape over and over and tell the nurses, doctors, and anyone who would listen that they needed to get born again. He said, "My son can tell you how to know if you are going to heaven when you die." Only God can change someone's heart, making him a new creature in Christ.

On the day of my brother's funeral, I was apprehensive about what I was going to say. I was even more apprehensive when I arrived at the funeral home. Outside around the hearse were about twenty members of the Hell's Angels motorcycle gang, all rigged out in their leather, sitting astride their Harley Davidson choppers. One of them had his head wrapped in a bandage where a bullet had grazed him in the drug raid where my brother had died. He was out of jail on bail. I motioned for them to come inside, and no one moved. I looked at them and said, "He was your friend in life, now come in and honor him in death." Hesitantly, they began to file in.

I walked down the aisle, and in the front row sat my mother with her leg in a cast from the beating David had given her. As I walked up to the casket, under my breath I asked the Holy Spirit to give me the words to say. Walking to the pulpit, He spoke to my heart saying, "Tell them there is a way that seems right to man, but the end thereof is the way to death." The Holy Spirit put one of the verses of Judges in my heart: *"Every man did that which was right in his own eyes"* (Judges 21:25 KJV). I told them that David had lived by that philosophy, and had died by that philosophy, and in a booming voice I said, "And he is in hell!"

You could have heard a pin drop. The funeral director got up and walked out. Some of the gang members started muttering and shifting around as if to challenge me. I jumped down from the pulpit to accept their challenge. I looked at them and said, "There is nothing I can do for David. I had told him about Jesus, and he made his choice." I told them David would go to a judgment called the Great White Throne Judgment, and one day David's soul would arise from the place of torment and be united with his body. He, along with all those who rejected Christ in this life, will stand before the throne at this judgment. The books will be opened, and they will be judged by the deeds done in this flesh.

And I saw the dead, small and great, stand before God; and the books were opened: and another book was opened, which is the book of life: and the dead were judged out of those things which were written in the books, according to their works.

And the sea gave up the dead which were in it; and death and hell delivered up the dead which were in them: and they were judged every man according to their works. And death and hell were cast into the lake of fire. This is the second death. And whosoever was not found written in the book of life was cast into the lake of fire. (Revelation 20:12–15 KJV)

What you have just read is the most sobering truth written anywhere in the Bible. The Great White Throne Judgment is an event so utterly awesome that all of creation trembles before it. Every non-believer will be there, both great and small, no matter what their status was in life. All who have died without Jesus Christ will face this final encounter. Isn't it ironic that the greatest fear of the unsaved is death, and it should be! They will also have to face the second death. God is always fair! And the Great White Throne Judgment is God's "double check," before they are cast into the lake of fire.

I then told them, "I know David. He's a con man, and he will try to con God. He'll say, 'Hey, God, I'm not a bad guy—I gave some money to my brother's church one time.' He will make up all kinds of excuses to try to justify all the things he has done. And with eyes full of sorrow, Jesus will say, 'David, I could have been your go-between, your lawyer, your mediator, but now I am your judge. You sealed your own fate with your rejection of my gift of salvation. You are sentenced to hell, for eternity!'" I stood there for a minute in silence and then looked at each person there and said, "It's not too late for you."

One of the gang members fell to his knees and began to cry, begging Jesus to forgive him. Then another and another followed. I went right down the line praying with each one as he gave his heart to Jesus. The funeral service had turned into a day of salvation. I looked up one time, and my mother was looking at me. I turned to her and said, "Mama, it's either life or death. You have one son who has gone to heaven and returned. You've got another son, you know what his lifestyle was like, and he is now dead. It is either heaven or hell, you have to choose." My mother replied, "Son, I want to go to heaven with you. Please, tell me about Jesus." Right there beside my brother's coffin, I led my mother to Jesus. Not long after David's funeral, my mother died. She has gone home to be with the Lord Jesus to that beautiful place called heaven.

> *Verily, verily, I say unto you, He that heareth my word, and believeth on him that sent me, hath everlasting life, and shall not come into condemnation; but is passed from death into life*
> (John 5:24 KJV)

If you are not saved, or if you have left the Lord, I pray that you will accept Jesus Christ as your personal Savior. You should determine today to make heaven the place where you will spend eternity. Remember, we are not promised a tomorrow. Right now, God wants to save you. He will never turn anyone away. *"For whosoever shall call upon the name of the Lord shall be saved"* (Romans 10:13 KJV).

Pray this prayer now:

Dear God,

I want to become a born-again Christian. I come to you in the name of Jesus, your son. I confess I am a sinner. I believe you sent your son to die on the cross for my sins. I confess with my mouth that Jesus Christ is Lord. Thank you for allowing me to become a Christian.

In Jesus' name I pray,

Amen!

A genuine born-again Christian wants, above everything else, to do the will of God. Don't be ashamed to witness to others and tell them how to become a Christian. Join a Bible-believing church and be water baptized as an act of faith to let the world know you are following Christ's example.

If you would like to receive the Holy Spirit, ask the Father in Jesus' name to fill you with the Holy Spirit. Believe you receive when you ask, and begin to speak your new language in faith as God gives it to you.

Repeat this prayer:

Father,

I come to you in faith, believing that Jesus Christ died in my place, for my sins, and arose from the dead. I ask you to fill me to overflowing with your Holy Spirit. You said in your Word that if I asked I would receive, so I ask you now to fill me to overflowing with your precious Holy Spirit. I receive Him now by faith and expect to speak with other tongues as He gives me the utterance.

In Jesus' name. Amen!

Now I want to pray for your healing. Put your hand on your body where you are sick and repeat this prayer: Lord Jesus you are the Great Physician. All healing comes from you. By your stripes we are healed. I speak your word over this body and thank you that you heal all our diseases. Thank you for healing and enabling me to walk in health.

In Jesus' Name Amen!

Letter of Authenticity:

I have known Gary, Deena, and Angel Wood for almost two decades. I came to know Gary through a mutual pastor friend who invited me to come hear his testimony of dying and going to heaven.

In my life, I have heard every type of that story that can be told. I sat out to find out everything about Gary that I could and prove him to be a fake.

In the two weeks after meeting Gary, I began an intense search into the man's background. There were several factors that brought me to my final answer.

1. The authorities in New Mexico verified the accident and fatality involved. Gary Lynn Wood was pronounced dead at the scene of the accident. The officer told me that it looked like they were going to have to hire someone just to take the calls inquiring about Mr. Wood. It was also told to me that the U.S. government has even investigated Mr. Wood to see if he was a con artist.

2. An employee of the hospital in Farmington, New Mexico, said that Gary had been without any vital signs for sixty-one minutes.

3. While making calls to find what I could about Gary's accident, he was in Jackson, Missouri, where he developed a throat problem. Mrs. Jean Seabough, a retired nurse, and I tried to get him to get medical attention as soon as possible. Gary did see a doctor in Rockford, Illinois. Three days later I was able to see the X-ray that was made at that visit to the doctor, proving to me that it is medically impossible for this man to talk, sing, walk, or even drink water. It is the same X-ray that he carries with him.

4. I have had people referred to me who were unable to be helped with medication. All of my patients go through a vast number of test and interviews. I invited Gary to come to Arkansas and visit with me and allow me to sit and talk to him about what he saw and went through from before the accident until he and Deena were married. This only brought more proof to me that everything he had said was truth.

There are many people since Gary's testimony has gone public who have made claim of visions and out of body experience, even deaths that were similar, but without proof of death. Gary has that proof.

Through all my investigating, questioning everyone I could, and talking person to person with Gary, with all the evidence my staff and I have found, to my knowledge there is only one man alive today that has proof positive that he actually died and went to heaven and returned to tell about it.

Dr. Gary L. Wood is without a doubt a true gift from the Lord to this generation. He was sent back to bring us a special message.

It is my honor to say Dr. Gary Wood is a close friend and an honest brother in the Lord.

Sincerely in Christ,

—Dr. Paul F. House, PhD, D.D., M.D.

To contact Evangelist Gary Wood about ministry or scheduling in your church please write or call:

Gary Wood Ministry
P.O. Box 1649
Sugar Land, TX 77487
Phone: (281) 491-4836
garywoodmi@aol.com
www.garywoodministries.com

Other Books by Gary Wood Ministries
Miracles: How to Get Your Miracle
Angel: A walking miracle. The story of Angel Wood's remarkable healing from mental retardation
Religion, Rebellion, Relationship: The story of David Wood
Born Again
Un Lugar LLamado Cielo

Order From:
Gary Wood Ministries
P.O. Box 1649
Sugarland, Texas 77487
garywoodmi@aol.com
www.garywoodministries.com

Photos

Ontario, Canada

Dr. Gary and Deena Wood

Dr. Gary, David, Shelley and Deena on David and Shelly's
Wedding Day. 3-1-08

Angel Wood

Dr. Gary and Deena Wood's Wedding Day
5-23-70

Gary and Deena's son David & wife Shelly

Dr. Gary, Deena, Billye Brim and Shelli Baggett

Deena, Angel and Deena's Parents
Ken and Louis Kennedy

Angel

Gary and Angel ministering at
Glorious Way Church
Houston, TX

Dr. Wood praying for people
Cornerstone Fellowship
Cobbs Creek, Virginia

Lining up for Dr. Gary to sign his book in Brazil

Revival in Ukraine

Life Church
Roscoe, IL